"If you're ready t[...]
have to liste[...]

**-James Malinchak - Featured on ABC's Hit TV Show
"Secret Millionaire," Two Time National College Speaker
Of The Year, Co-Author of Chicken Soup For The
College Soul, And Found of BigMoneySpeaker.com**

*"Mike Fritz can show any student how to become a
leader and make a **REAL** difference on campus."*

**-Jonathan Sprinkles, APCA National
College Speaker of the Year**

*"Mike's leadership strategies are exactly what students need
to hear to start leading and making impact immediately."*

**-Joe Martin - APCA National College Speaker
of the Year, creator of TricksoftheGrade.com
and America's #1 Educator Motivator**

*"Mike is the funniest guy you will ever meet and a wonderful
speaker on leadership. He knows how to make learning about
leadership fun. Read this book if you are ready to lead well.*

**- Paul Prestwich President of North West
College and National Author and Speaker**

*"Mike Fritz shares a wonderful blend of humor and insight
in Great Student Leaders Aren't Born They're Made. This
must have book is not just a one-and-doe read. Keep this one-
of-a-kind book close by and refer to its inspiration often"*

**-Matt Patterson, Speaker/Author of Award Winning
Amazon Best Seller, "My Emily", mattpaterson.me**

"Mike is a genius! His book Great Student Leaders Aren't Born There Made is a roadmap to success for every student who chooses to embrace Mike's thoughts. Through story and humor Mike leads the reader thru key elements that unlocks unlimited possibilities. This is a must-read for any student (or anyone for that matter) who desires to become the leader they were meant to be. I highly recommend this book and Mike!!"

- Gary Barnes- The #1 Traction Coach in America, www.GaryBarnesinternational.com

"The most important choice that a leader makes is the decision to embrace the leader within. Mike Fritz's leadership strategies, presented in his humorous and down-to-earth fashion, is a quick read filled with timeless leadership lessons."

-Virginia Barkley, #1 Best-Selling Author, ClutterBusting For Busy Women; How To Create A C.A.L.M. Life to Have More Time & Energy, www.VirginiaBarkley.com

"This book by Mike Fritz is phenomenal His 52 tips can help any leader from entry level all the way up to upper executives. He is an amazing author and a great speaker"

-John Salkowski, Founder of Achieve Success Academy adn author of the "Leading in the Line of Duty" series.

GREAT
STUDENT LEADERS
AREN'T BORN
THEY'RE MADE

52 Tips for Leading Yourself, Others and Your Student Organization

Published by Mike Fritz Communications, Inc.

Copyright © 2013 Mike Fritz Communications, Inc

Printed in the United States of America

ISBN: 978-0615745848

Mike Fritz Communications:
Great Student Leaders Are Not Born They Are Made by Mike
Fritz

Disclaimer/Warning:
This book is intended for lecture and entertainment purposes
only. The author or publisher does not guarantee that anyone
following these steps will be a successful leader. The author
and publisher shall have neither liability responsibility to
anyone with respect to any loss or damage cause, or alleged to
be caused, directly or indirectly by the information contained
in this book.

GREAT
STUDENT LEADERS
AREN'T BORN
THEY'RE MADE

52 Tips for Leading Yourself, Others and Your Student Organization

MIKE FRITZ
America's Funniest Leadership Speaker

ABOUT MIKE:

Mike has delivered over 1,000 motivating presentations all over the country at colleges, conferences, schools and other meetings. He has a background in standup comedy and leadership training. He decided to mend his two passions together and has become *America's Funniest Leadership Speaker.* Students, business owners, teachers and many others have enjoyed Mike's life changing and hilarious lessons on leadership.

Mike's passion for leadership came early in his speaking career when he continually heard people say things like "you are either born a leader or not." This is what he was told as a young student in high school. He was told many times he wasn't born to be a leader. Mike's hilarious and inspiring story of how he "decided" to be a leader will challenge you, make you cry and make you laugh all in one message.

Mike is one of the most dynamic young speakers on the speaking circuit today. He has the ability to connect with audiences of any age while making specific life applications so that people know what to do when they leave his session. His goal is to inspire the leader within all of us. He believes we were all created to lead; but it is our choice.

For more resources and to subscribe to Mike's free newsletter "Leader by Choice" go to Mike's website www.mikefritz.net

Mike Fritz
America's Funniest Leadership Speaker

INTRODUCTION

Leadership is quite possibly the most sought after skill in the world. In the last year U.S companies have increased 14% in their spending on leadership training for their employees. This is a huge increase. Look at these numbers. Per year companies are spending:

$1,671 per person per year for 1st level leaders

$2,700 per person per year for Midlevel leaders

$6,016 per person per year for Senior leaders

$7,116 per person per year for High potentials

These are staggering numbers. Why are companies pouring so much money into the area of leadership? Because leaders are what make businesses successful. Leaders are what make businesses money. As John Maxwell says, "Everything rises and falls on leadership."

I grew up being told that leaders were born. People are either leaders or they aren't. It isn't your choice. You don't choose leadership, leadership chooses you. This, however, is false. My purpose in this book is to give you 52 tips that can turn you or anyone else into a leader. I am living proof that anyone can be a leader.

As you continue to read beware! These tips will put 100% of the responsibility of leadership in your lap. It will remove all excuses and give you the tools to start leading today in your school, in your dorm, on your team, at home or anywhere else. Read at your own risk. With these tips you can change the world!

Tip #1:
LEADERSHIP STARTS WITH YOU

Leadership is an internal decision that produces external results. You must first understand that no matter who you are, you *can* lead. Leadership is much more about what you do than what personality you have. Leading is a choice that starts with you. You will never be able to lead and influence people until you are first taking the steps you wish to see others take. What do you believe others need to do to be successful? Are you doing them? Let's get to work!

> "You Can Only Lead Others Where
> You Yourself Are Willing To Go."
> **—LACHLAN MCLEAN**

Tip #2:

GREAT STUDENT LEADERSHIP IS NOT A SPECTATOR SPORT

I am a huge San Francisco 49ers fan. A few years ago my wife bought me tickets to see them play the Cincinnati Bengals for my birthday. While I was at the game, I overheard a man that was well over 350 pounds critiquing the players on their performance. Here was a fat, undisciplined "bleacher-sitter" telling world famous athletes how to play more effectively. In fact, one time he screamed, "Get off your butt and do something you lazy bum." Mind you, he had what I am sure was an entire bag of potato chips in his mouth when he screamed this. I got the inclination he would have washed it down with a glass of gravy as though it were a beverage had it been available.

It is so easy to critique those who are leading and seeking to make things happen. Leaders don't simply sit back and critique but seek to learn from those in leadership; they want to learn both from what leaders are doing well and what they are doing poorly. Leaders don't watch others make it happen; they participate in making things happen. Are you seeking to influence people, or are you critiquing the influencers around you, like our football friend?

> "Leaders don't watch others
> do; they take action."
> — **MIKE FRITZ**

Tip #3:

GREAT STUDENT LEADERS: DOGS OR CATS?

I hate all animals. Relax I am just...well, no, it's actually true. I really don't like them. I once had a man tell me, with tears in his eyes, "When I get home it is so nice to have my little Ruffy, who doesn't judge me and meets me with uncontrolled excitement."

I thought to myself, "This guy has a family; his wife and kids don't give him that type of affirmation - its a good thing too; that would be kind of creepy, if the kids came up and started licking the guy's face."

While it would be a little – or a lot! – weird if we humans greeted one another with a lick on the face, let's think about our animal friends and the lessons we can learn from them. Dogs and cats are completely different. Dogs serve you and make a big deal when you get home and come running to the door to greet you. Cats just sit there and silently seem to say, "It's about time your home. I need some food." Dogs make a big deal, cats say "big deal." Dogs exist to serve you and cats exist to give you the opportunity to serve them. Which one are you? Are you a dog or cat? Do you primarily serve people or do you wait to be served? Leaders are constantly looking for ways to serve and enrich the lives of those around them. Nothing will add more followers (and I'm not talking about Twitter for any computer gurus out there) than your willingness to be a servant leader (a leader who meets the needs of others).

"Leadership is always built
upon service and sacrifice."
- JAMES C. HUNTER

Tip #4:
GREAT STUDENT LEADERS ARE SOLUTION CONSCIOUS NOT EXCUSE CONSCIOUS.

"When you blame others you forfeit your ability to change."

-DR. ROBERT ANTHONY

Have you ever encountered someone that had an excuse for everything? We learn excuse making at an early age, don't we? You can see this with children fighting? If one kid hits another and then the kid that was hit retaliates and hits back, and you were to walk up to him and say to the retaliator, "Why did you hit him?" you can almost be guaranteed he will say, "Because he hit me first." It is as if we are born avoiding responsibility. It never crossed the kid's mind that he didn't *have* to retaliate. But excuse making is ingrained in us. What would you think if you walked up to that retaliator and said, "Why did you hit him?" and he responded, "Well I am 100% in control of my actions, so the reason I did that was that I really wanted him to feel the same pain that he just inflicted on me. So to answer your question...I hit him for revenge. I probably should be punished."

Have you ever received a poor grade on a paper or test? Did you ever blame the teacher? "He/she didn't tell us we had to know that." Mr. So And So never explains it in a way that I can understand it." Mrs. So And So just doesn't like me." These are some of the excuses I used when I failed. But I later realized leaders don't look for excuses; they look for solutions. Next time you face a tough situation, instead of finding a way to make it someone else's fault, look for a way to make the situation better.

> "When a leader falls he is
> not a failure until he blames
> someone for pushing him."
> **- MIKE FRITZ**

Tip #5:

GREAT STUDENT LEADERS UNDERSTAND THE POWER OF LEADERSHIP AND DON'T MISUSE IT.

> "Nearly all men can stand adversity,
> but if you want to test a man's
> character, give him power."
>
> **- ABRAHAM LINCOLN**

Some of us don't understand how much power we possess when we lead. It can be like a bazooka in the hand of a baby. I had a friend named Scott when I was growing up. He had just received a 12-gauge shot gun for Christmas. He loaded it one day and shot a few shells but didn't know that there was one more in the chamber. He put his gun away. A week later he picked it up and was carrying it around. He had no idea of the power he held in his hand - and what a danger it could be if misused. He had been watching too many Sylvester Stallone and Jason Statham movies and he looked into a mirror and said, "You are dead" and pulled the trigger. He blew a hole in the side of his house about the size of a soccer ball. He was upstairs when he did this while his mom was downstairs making dinner. She was of course scared half to death by the gun shot and screamed up the stairs, "What was that?" Scott, not thinking very clearly, said, "Uh...nothing." As if she was going to just say, "Okay" and go back to cooking! This story has amused me for years. He had a gun but had no idea of its power at that particular moment. As leaders we must understand the power of leadership. Because of the nature of its power it can be used to bring countries to freedom, free thousands of tortured slaves or bring terrorists to justice. However it also has the power to enslave and brainwash people like Hitler and Stalin did. It is quite possibly the most powerful tool on the planet.

> ## "Leadership is quite possibly the most powerful tool on the planet"
> ### - MIKE FRITZ

Tip #6:

GREAT STUDENT LEADERS HAVE A SPOTTER

I played football in high school, which is hard to believe if you know that I weighed about 135 pounds back then. I was a wide receiver. I was so small I looked like a bunch of twigs tied together and then given a pulse. My uncle once lifted my arm up and said "That is the longest wrist I have ever seen". My wrist and my bicep were the same size. One summer vacation my football coach was trying to help me bulk up and put me on a weight lifting routine. I went to the gym every day. One day I was working on my bench pressing. Those of you that work out know what a spotter is; for those of you who don't: a spotter is someone who stands behind the bar and makes sure you can get the bar back up to its rest so it doesn't come crashing down on you if your strength gives out. One day I was in the weight room alone and I was lifting a fairly heavy weight for me (which wasn't much). I got to the 6th repetition and I couldn't get the bar up. As slow as I could I lowered the bar down on my chest...which wasn't slow at all considering it bounced. So there I was with the bar pinning me to the bench, with no one in the weight room to help me and no way to get myself out of this predicament. So I did what any other desperate twig man would do in this situation. I tilted my body so the weights would slide off one side, which they did; then the bar, of course, was yanked at the speed of light to the other side with the weights still on it, and those weights fell off. There I laid. My chest felt cracked...weights all over...breathing like I was in labor. Why? It was all because I didn't have a spotter to help me. All leaders need help. If you are trying to lead by yourself, you will only go so far. Choose a person today that you can ask to help you become a better leader.

"Leaders are following leaders"
- **MIKE FRITZ**

Tip #7:
GREAT STUDENT LEADERS ARE ORIGINAL

> "Everyone is born an original
> but most become a copy"
> **- GABRIEL COUSENS**

I have worked with high school and college students for almost a decade. Every day I see students that are doing everything they can to be someone else because they are dissatisfied with who they are. I hear people talk like other people, dress like other people, and walk like other people. I even see adults trying to act like teenagers just to try to relate. It is hilarious seeing a 40 year old trying to dress and act like Justin Bieber. But isn't this true all over the place? We see people trying to be like other people all the time. And I guess if you went on a date and were completely yourself it might be taken the wrong way. Like if you are someone who doesn't hold back and tells the truth, and your date walks up and you say, "Wow, you chose to wear that? I totally mean to hurt you by saying this: it makes you look fat and ugly. But in all seriousness, your shoes are great." That level of openness could get you in trouble. In all seriousness, be YOU! You are the only thing that makes you different from everyone else.

> ## "YOU are the only YOU this world has. Don't rob us of YOU."
> ### - MIKE FRITZ

Tip #8:

GREAT STUDENT LEADERS SEE FAILURE AS BUILDING BLOCKS FOR SUCCESS

"Hardship often prepares an ordinary person for an extraordinary destiny"

- CS LEWIS

The first time I went snow skiing was one of the funniest things to watch according to my un-athletic, never-play-a-sport-in-his- life uncle. In his words my body looked like "two detached spaghetti noodles." I finally learned how to stay up on my skis long enough to make it down the bunny hill; however, by the time I got to the bottom I was traveling at the speed of a bullet - or at least that's how it felt. The discovery I made at the bottom of the hill is that I didn't know how to stop. Inconveniently I figured this out after

I had reached the top speed that my body had ever traveled while mounted on two fiberglass sticks. So at my peak speed I was heading straight for the storage shed. Why any ski resort would think that at the bottom of the bunny hill was a good place to put the storage shed is far beyond my comprehension but some executives apparently thought this would help people. This painful experience taught me I needed to learn to stop. Slamming into a building will do that to you. Both my skis came off, I lost both my poles and both of my already exhausted knees slammed into the shed. As I was lying in the rubble of my equipment I thought to myself, "I need to learn to stop".

This incident and my first day skiing was the first day of an eight year journey. I fell more times than you can imagine while I was learning. However, every time I fell I learned something: how to not fall the next time. Eight years later I was skiing in the Rocky Mountains through the trees, jumping off cliffs and having a blast. It was one of the most fun things I have ever done. Had I not learned from falling I would have missed out on the victory of skiing in Colorado. Failure can be a great teacher if you're willing to be taught. Failure often crushes people because they don't see it as a teacher; they see it as the enemy. The next time you fail say this (out loud): "What have I or can I learn that will make me better than I ever could have been had this not happened?"

> "Failure is the opportunity to
> begin again more intelligently"
> **- HENRY FORD**

Tip #9:

GREAT STUDENT LEADERS USE WORDS THAT MOTIVATE

When I was in 8th grade I played tight end for our school's football team. We were in a close game one night and a play was called in which the ball would be thrown to me. The ball was hiked and I went out for the pass. As I was running the quarterback launched it into the air and it was about 15 yards past where I could get to it. But to show the coach that I was a dedicated player I heaved myself into the air - diving for the ball. It was a bit embarrassing when I landed and then the ball landed 15 yards beyond me. However that wasn't even the most embarrassing part. When I landed my pants came down all the way around my knees. We had a pretty big school so there were a lot of people in the stands. To my horror I realized that it wasn't just my pants that came down; that's right...there I laid in my birthday suit in front of all those people 15 yards away from the ball. My coach came up to me with a ticked off look on his face and I thought to myself, "Oh here we go; he is going to chew me out." To my surprise he said, "That is what I am looking for Fritz." I thought to myself, "What? A tight end diving for a ball he can't catch and having his pants come down?" I never forgot that because it made me feel like I could do anything. The very next play they threw it to me again and I caught it and ran it down to the 3 yard line. Leaders use words that motivate.

"Motivating others at its most
fundamental level IS leadership"
- MIKE FRITZ

Tip #10:

GREAT STUDENT LEADERS DON'T TEAR DOWN; THEY SHARE DOWN

Has anyone ever shared his dream with you and you thought to yourself (or maybe you even said it), "Man, you aren't going to be able to do that. That is way too unrealistic." What if every time someone shared his goal with you, you gave him any help you could so that he could go pursue it. Are you known for encouraging people to pursue their dreams? Have you ever succeeded at anything? Don't say no; everyone has succeeded at something. What made it possible for you to succeed? Maybe it was a good coach, or teacher or counselor, or friend, or hard work, or a specific strategy you used; whatever it may have been, that is what others need to hear about. You know what business coaching is? It's sharing with others what made you successful or perhaps even things that you tried that didn't work but you learned from. Share something with someone in the next 24 hours that will help them achieve their goals.

"Before you are a leader, success is all about growing yourself. When you become a leader, success is all about growing others."

- JACK WELCH

Tip #11:

GREAT STUDENT LEADERS WILL LEARN FROM ANYONE

Have you ever met that annoying person that always seems to have advice for others, even though they don't seem to follow their own advice? You know, the fitness trainer that is 100 pounds overweight, or the marriage counselor that has kids that most likely will grow up to be terrorists. Before you write off these little bundles of unseen blessing, think about it from a different perspective. Imagine if every time they open their annoying mouth they presented you with a free opportunity to grow. Their annoying advice could actually be fuel for your success. I have learned things from 6 year olds and 80 year olds. Leaders are more concerned about learning and getting better than they are about who is teaching them.

> "It is sometimes unsolicited advice
> that produces the most fertile
> soil for growth and progress"
>
> **- MIKE FRITZ**

Tip #12:
GREAT STUDENT LEADERS ARE FOREVER IMPROVING

The fact that you are reading this right now is proof that you are a leader. The fact that you want tips to becoming a better leader is what will eventually make you a great leader. The moment you stop growing and changing is the moment that you are rendered useless as a leader. Never stop reading good books, listening to great speakers and teachers and asking questions from experts. These are the steps that every leader makes. You show me a leader, and I will show you someone that is improving constantly.

Challenge: Read 10 minutes when you get up and 10 minutes before you go to bed every day. In 20 minutes a day, your life can change. Never stop learning!

"You may only be 20 minutes away
from being a great leader"

- MIKE FRITZ

Tip #13:

GREAT STUDENT LEADERS LEAD, THEY DON'T FOLLOW THE FAILURE CROWD

I know this may initially seem obvious, but it's not. Just because people have told you that you are a leader doesn't mean you are. Very few people relentlessly pursue their dreams. Many people are following people that aren't even successful. Leaders evaluate who they are following and ask whether they are going in the direction they want to go. But more importantly, leaders are following their own dreams. I have decided that I will only follow those who will help me pursue my dreams with greater purpose and intensity.

When I was eleven years old I was at my friend's house playing video games. I don't know if you have a friend that isn't smart enough to say, "That is a dumb idea...we can't do that" when you come up with a dumb idea. I had many friends like that growing up. This one was one of them. After a while we got tired of playing video games and he said, "Dude lets go get up on top of my garage and jump off the roof into the pool." To which I responded, "Heck yeah...lets go." There was a ladder leaned up against the roof and he climbed up it and got on the roof. I climbed up the ladder but stayed on it to see what happened to him before I got up there. What you need to know about this roof is that it had holes in it all over the place... that were big enough to fall through. But he jumped over them like it was nothing and jumped into the unknown...for a second I couldn't hear anything and then splash - he landed safely. I guess now it was my turn. So I got up on the roof from the ladder. There were three holes in between me and liquid bliss. I jumped over the first one...success. I jumped over the second one...success. One more to go. I jumped over the third one, but didn't quite make it and fell all the way through the roof into the garage – oh, but don't worry; the rototiller broke my fall. So there I was, lying in the garage on the concrete floor with a gouge in my back from bouncing off the rototiller and thinking to myself, "I should have led through that a bit better instead of following the crowd." You must remember, a leader leads and doesn't follow the crowd. Often the crowd is not going in the right direction.

> "A man who wants to lead the orchestra must turn his back on the crowd."
>
> **- MAX LUCADO**

Tip #14:
GREAT STUDENT LEADERS VALUE THEIR TIME

Have you ever asked someone what he was doing and he said, "Oh...just killing some time"? Right now, today, strike that phrase from your vocabulary. Time is the only thing you have. Every success and dream you have needs time to come to fruition. Every relationship you want to build needs time. Every goal you have needs time to achieve. What do you want out of this life? Without time you have nothing. Don't kill time; rather, seize time and use it to serve as many people as you can and achieve as many goals as your mind can conceive.

Beware of people who waste your time. In may not be their intention, but if you let them, they will rob you of your life. I was sitting with one of my mentors one time and as I was leaving I said, "Thanks so much for your time." To which he responded, "I didn't give you time. I gave you my life." We all only have so much life and every second we are investing it in something. What or who are you investing your life (time) into?

"Every second that passes is one that can never be relived. Use time wisely."

- MIKE FRITZ

Tip #15:
GREAT STUDENT LEADERS ARE GRATEFUL

I grew up in a home where my parents blessed me with innumerable material possessions. I got a brand new pickup truck when I was 16 and another new one when I turned 18. Most people can't imagine that. However, even after my parents were so generous, I went to school with a few people that had an even nicer vehicle than I had and I was still ungrateful. Throughout my life, as my parents blessed me over and over again, I began to treat them as vehicles to get what I wanted rather than people that I could serve and whose lives I could enrich.

My wife has taught me more about being grateful than anyone on earth. She didn't grow up with near as much as I did. She was so thankful for everything that was in her life. She taught me the power in writing thank you notes. She taught me that just saying "thank you" doesn't mean you are grateful. She taught me that gratitude is much more about the way you view people than what you say. I can truly say that I am grateful for my wife. Leaders must be grateful. People are much more likely to follow leaders that appreciate them than those that seem to take their followers for granted. Who has played a role in you getting to where you are? Your parents, coaches, aunts, uncles, grandparents, friends, teachers, or neighbors? Let them know how they have impacted you today by sending them an email, writing a thank you note or giving them a call.

"Gratitude is not only the greatest of virtues, but the parent of all others."
– MARCUS TULLIUS CICERO

Tip #16:

GREAT STUDENT LEADERS SACRIFICE FOR OTHERS

Maybe you have heard the story of the mom that was making pancakes for her boys one morning. The two boys were sitting at the table arguing over who would get to eat the first pancake. The older said, "I am older. I have earned the right to have the first pancake." To which the younger replied, "I am the youngest, you should let me have the pancake." The mom, seeing this as a great opportunity to teach, used Jesus as an example. She said, "You know boys, Jesus would let his brother have the pancake." To that, the older brother looked at the younger brother and said, "You be Jesus."

Laying aside your own desires to serve those under your leadership is quite possibly the greatest of leadership tips. Those on your team and thus under your care are not steps to getting what you want, but rather objects of your love, teaching and service.

> "The first question which the priest and the Levite asked was: 'If I stop to help this man, what will happen to me?' But...the good Samaritan reversed the question: 'If I do not stop to help this man, what will happen to him?'"
>
> **- MARTIN LUTHER**

Tip #17:

GREAT STUDENT LEADERS ASK QUESTIONS AND SEEK CLARIFICATION RATHER THAN MAKE ACCUSATIONS

Have you ever made a judgment about someone based only on assumptions or hearsay? Have you ever accused someone of something only to find out later you were wrong? Have you ever had someone say something to you and you totally misinterpreted what they said because you judged their intentions? I do this to my wife all the time. She says something, I misinterpret it and respond based upon my own misinterpretation rather than on her intention and meaning. Why would anyone want to believe something that isn't true like that? Most of the time it is because we believe we know what a person meant even if he or she tells us otherwise. It is almost as if we want to have something on them...maybe to make us feel better or bigger. However, when someone says something that seems to rub you wrong ask a question: "Hey what did you mean by that?" When someone does something that seems totally incorrect ask them why they did it that way. Don't assume you know. Accusations can alienate people and rarely, if ever, encourage and motivate change.

"Questions stir the mind but accusations harden the will"

- KEN COLLIER

Tip# 18:
GREAT STUDENT LEADERS LOSE THE EGO

Have you ever seen the commercials for Eggo Waffles? Someone would be toasting a waffle and someone else would come by and steal it just as it popped from the toaster. The person who was making the waffle was totally upset that someone would have the audacity to steal their piece of bread with imprinted boxes in it. Sometimes that is the way we act when we don't get the credit that we think we deserve.

Leaders are more concerned about success as a whole than they are about people acknowledging their part in smaller successes. Leaders are constantly seeking to lose the ego. Ego is that immaterial part in us that cries out for recognition and credit. Leaders make their mission much less about themselves and much more about the people following their leadership and the people they are helping.

> "If I have seen further than others, it is by standing upon the shoulders of giants."
>
> **- ISAAC NEWTON**

Tip #19:
GREAT STUDENT LEADERS VALUE DIVERSITY

I love it when people disagree with me. My favorite part is when my blood pressure gets so high you can see the veins in my neck pop out. Then always follows the things you say that you really regret later. My wife and I were arguing one day with all our might. I was seeking to help her see my brilliance, but it just wasn't working. Some people just don't appreciate perfection...and if you buy that as the country music writer said, "I'll throw the Golden Gate in free." Do you value people that differ from you? I'm not talking about race, gender or ethnicity. I'm referring to people with different perspectives. I have found that the reason that I hate it when people disagree with me is because I want to be perceived as the expert; and when people disagree with me I think they are challenging my expertise. How foolish this is. Disagreement is often the greatest opportunity to learn and grow. But most people are infatuated with being right rather than learning and growing. Leaders value differing opinions. The more I listen to those that disagree with me the more I grow as a leader. Often times in leadership it isn't that someone is right and wrong, it is just a difference in opinion. A leader's job is to listen and choose the best perceived direction based upon what can be known about the issues at hand.

> ## "In the gathering of multiple perspectives giants are born"
> ### - MIKE FRITZ

Tip #20:

GREAT STUDENT LEADERS REJOICE AT THE SUCCESS OF OTHERS

It sounded like nails on a chalk board when his name was called for the award that was supposed to go to me. It was the 4th grade student of the month. I was spitting angry. How could any teacher miss the amazing Fritz-charm that wandered the halls each day. I mean, if there is one thing that teachers should learn in college it is how to identify those that truly DESERVE student of the month.

I don't know about you but jumping up and down when others succeed is hard for me. I would much rather "weep with those that weep" than "rejoice with those that rejoice." The truth is leaders aren't threatened by others' success, but are liberated by it unto their own greatness. The next time someone in your sphere of influence succeeds, don't become threatened, but rather encourage them.

"The people who are lifting the world onward and upward are those who encourage more than they criticize."
– ELIZABETH HARRISON

Tip #21:

GREAT STUDENT LEADERS STUDY HOW PEOPLE THINK AND WHAT MOTIVATES THEM

The more you understand how people work the better you are going to lead. The most important thing to know about people is that they make decisions based upon their mind, will and emotions. If you want to influence someone you must first help change their thinking enough so that they see the benefit in following you. That is the most powerful thing I use in my speaking and coaching. Although people have different styles, personalities and preferences they all follow certain patterns. You must understand what motivates them to do a great job; knowing this, you can customize the way you work with them to optimize their productivity and enjoyment.

"You must trade minds with the people you want to influence"

- DAVID SCHWATZ

Tip #22:

GREAT STUDENT LEADERS DON'T SET LIMITS THEY SET GOALS

There are two ways to approach success: through limits or through goals. You can set goals based on what you think you can achieve or you can set goals based upon what you want to achieve. Most people set limits rather than goals. In their mind there is a pre-conceived limit that they can't go beyond, therefore they set their goals just before those limits to avoid failure. This is what we call a "limiting belief." We need what I call "goal beliefs" - beliefs that are attached to our goals. We have all, at one time or another, believed lies about our abilities. Someone told me, "I don't see you as the funny speaker." I wanted to graciously and loving take his hot coffee and dump it over his head. A funny speaker is what

I wanted to be. So he was in essence telling me that I wasn't good at the very thing I wanted to do...and this was from a friend! I had a decision to make regarding what I wanted to do in my mind with this discouraging statement. I slowly began setting goals based upon what I thought I could achieve rather than what I wanted to achieve, until one day I was speaking and numerous people came up to me and said the opposite. I thought to myself, "Why am I giving this one guy's view of me so much power in my mind?" I gave this person's view so much power because it was a doubt I had in my own mind. I would say to myself, "Can I really be America's Funniest Leadership Speaker?" Then when he essentially said "no," I believed it. When you set limits in your mind and others validate them it makes these limits that much harder to overcome. Set goals, not limits.

"Leaders only have the limits they place upon themselves"
- MIKE FRITZ

Tip #23:

GREAT STUDENT LEADERS BUILD RELATIONSHIPS

"You manage things, you lead people"

- REAR ADMIRAL GRACE MURRAY HOPPER

Relationships are foundational to leadership. People will only follow someone for so long unless they know that their leader cares for them and they can trust that the leader has their best interest at heart. My JV basketball coach was one of the most caring people I have ever met. He was my favorite coach of all the coaches I have ever had. The reason I played so hard for him and would have tried anything on the court that he asked me to do was that I knew that he cared about me as a person and wanted to see me become successful. He was so impactful he was an honored guest at my wedding. What a great man.

Being a leader means that you are pursuing deep relationships.

"You need to care for people before you can properly lead them"

- MIKE FRITZ

Tip #24:

GREAT STUDENT LEADERS MASTERMIND AND SPEND TIME WITH OTHER LEADERS

"When spiders unite they
can tie up a lion"

ETHIOPIAN PROVERB

Who is on your leadership team that is making you a better leader by critiquing your leadership so that you can improve? Getting critiqued can be like getting a root canal - not fun. I was sitting in the chair getting a root canal one time; the dentist put his hand in my mouth and then wanted to have a conversation with me. Try that just for fun. Put your hand in your mouth (come on do it) and then try to say, "My name is _____." It's not easy is it? What is wrong with these dentists? Anyway, I had a dead tooth that needed to be fixed. It was starting to affect the teeth around it. So the dentist said we need to fix this so that the rest of the teeth aren't impacted by this tooth's poor health. Your leadership is this way. If you have an area of your leadership that needs to change and you don't realize it, it could be impacting and sabotaging the rest of your leadership impact. We need people that can objectively look at our leadership and prod us along now and then. Every good leader gets evaluated for the sake of greatness.

> "It is the areas of your life you don't see that are most clearly seen by others."
> **- MIKE FRITZ**

Tip #25:
GREAT STUDENT LEADERS SPEAK TRUTH

"Don't sugar coat things, it will rot the teeth of those that eat your words"
- UNKNOWN

You ever have someone say, "I tell it like it is" as they bob their head from side to side like a bobble head doll and at the same time wave just one finger in the air? Never understood why just one finger, but nonetheless, don't confuse this with leadership. Leaders say what NEEDS to be said WHEN it needs to be said HOW it needs to be said. It is that person that is willing to speak up for the group. You must remember there is always hope in the truth. It is only when we hear and understand the truth that we can optimally perform. Don't be afraid to diplomatically state truth. Don't be afraid to go against the grain and bring up something that no one else is saying.

"The truth is inconvertible, malice may attack it, ignorance may deride it, but in the end it is there to help"

- WINSTON CHURCHILL

Tip #26:

GREAT STUDENT LEADERS ARE PEACEMAKERS

A LESSON FROM CHILDREN

Peacemaking is the desire and ability to resolve conflict quickly and effectively. Most people in leadership positions are more concerned with "Peace-faking". Peace-faking is when everyone fakes like there is no problem and appears to move on even though they may be fuming or hurt on the inside. Have you ever seen a young child hit another kid. You walk up to them and say, "Don't hit him (of course lets just assume it is two young boys), say you're sorry." So the little boy with darts in is forehead and a scowl on his face says, "Im sorry." Is there peace between the two parties? Or was a child forced to mouth words? Too often that is the way we lead. Relational problems have ruined families, companies, sports teams, bands, pick up games etc. If this can be such an issue, the leader must understand how to address conflict.

"Relationships will only be as deep as people's ability to make peace through conflict resolution."

- MIKE FRITZ

Tip #27:

GREAT STUDENT LEADERS ARE PURPOSE DRIVEN RATHER THAN RESULTS DRIVEN

"Purpose is the most dependable vehicle to get you to your desired destination"

- MIKE FRITZ

Aren't results the reason you are leading? Yes! However, if results are your only motivator, what happens when you don't get the result you want? Many people are tempted to quit. Jack Canfield and Mark Victor Hansen, authors of the bestselling book series, "Chicken Soup for the Soul" went to 144 publishers before a publisher took a chance on them by publishing their book. Imagine if they were results driven *only*. After time 12...26...59...71...97...1 15...129...131...do you think that they were tempted to quit? Several publishers told them that the book idea was stupid and that people wouldn't buy it. But, they weren't focused on the results as much as their purpose for writing this book. Their purpose was to uplift and encourage people through short but meaningful stories. Purpose keeps you going when the results have not yet come. Leaders are motivated by their own purpose and they also motivate others by keeping their purpose in mind. Make sure you focus on the purpose you have in school...working at your job...in a certain relationship...it will take you through the times when the results seem distant and the struggle doesn't seem worth it.

> "Purpose keeps you going when
> the results have not yet come."
> **- MIKE FRITZ**

Tip #28:
GREAT STUDENT LEADERS HAVE HIGH INTEGRITY

"A man will gladly die for
another that he can trust"

- TONY DUNGY

Have you ever met someone that would lie even if the truth sounded better? I had a friend like that in school. It simply became known that any word that came out of his mouth should be held in suspect. He came in one morning to school and swore a deer jumped OVER his car. Now, I'm not saying that's impossible, but he lived in the city with no woods in sight for about 20 miles. Another time he swore he got a date with this girl that was good looking enough to be a supermodel. We asked her, "Hey, did you go on a date with (my friend's name)?" To which she replied, "who?" If you are going to lead with any sort of effectiveness you are going to have to lead with honesty. I have seen dishonesty ruin marriages, other relationships, businesses, teams, and beyond.

WAYS PEOPLE DEMONSTRATE LOW INTEGRITY:

Buy one CD and then copy it to give to many other people. Imagine if you were the artist; what would you want?

Telling a teacher your printer broke and you couldn't print your paper, when your printer is actually fine; you just didn't get the paper done.

Borrowing money and having to be asked several times to pay it back

These are just a few ways we lie. Leaders lead with integrity.

> "Dishonesty is the erosion that eats at the foundation of your leadership"
> **- MIKE FRITZ**

Tip #29:

GREAT STUDENT LEADERS DON'T CUT CORNERS.

It was said of Dave Thomas, the founder of the fast food restaurant Wendy's, that the reason that Wendy's burgers were square was because Dave didn't want to cut corners. He said, "Every other burger joint has round burgers." I guess he was the first to "Think outside the bun" no matter what Taco Bell says. Cutting corners usually comes from a desire to skip the hard work and simply get to the results. I am all for getting to the results as quickly as possible. However, while quality isn't more important than quantity necessarily, quality does create more quantity over time. I have seen so many "Get rich quick" programs in my time. I was even sucked into buying one off an infomercial one time. The problem with get rich quick programs is that they create the perception that you don't have to work for the results. I do think there are things you can do to speedily build wealth, but not outside of the context of hard, consistent, persistent work.

> "It all comes back to the basics. Serve customers the best-tasting food at a good value in a clean, comfortable restaurant, and they'll keep coming back."
>
> **- DAVE THOMAS**

Tip #30:
GREAT STUDENT LEADERS LISTEN

"When you talk you put your learning on hold, unless you are asking questions"
- MIKE FRITZ

I love to talk. In fact, I have been told that I am pretty good at it by a number of people. I often find myself in meetings, events and conversations where people are asking for my perspective. I don't like to listen that much...because the truth is if other people are talking instead of me, their life can't be changed by my unbelievable wisdom and knowledge. We would never word it that way, but often that is the way we think. Have you ever met someone that interrupts other people all the time? Often, the reason people do that is because they believe that what they have to say is more important than what the other person is trying to communicate. When you talk, you can't learn from others. When you talk, your own learning is on hold. Leaders must learn the art of listening. Don't interrupt people. When people are talking engage in what they are saying by looking at them, resist thinking about your response before they are even finished speaking, ask questions to make sure you understand them, and ignore your phone if you get a text or notification unless you have a potential emergency.

"Be quick to listen and slow to speak"
JAMES 1:19

Tip #31:

GREAT STUDENT LEADERS DON'T WAIT FOR OPPORTUNITIES TO COME THEIR WAY

> "Things may come to those who wait, but only the things left over by those who hustle"
>
> **- ABRAHAM LINCOLN**

When I was in high school, I played cornerback on our football team. One Friday night during a game, the other team was in the middle of a pass play. After the receiver caught the ball I stood still waiting for him to get to me rather than bolting ahead toward him to avoid getting run past. While I was standing there one of the other team's players blindsided and crushed me, launching my 130 pound body into flight. When I was in the air I had no contact with planet earth. At the end of that experience I was laying on the ground in pain as our rival's receiver pranced himself on to a touchdown. I learned an important leadership tip from that experience. Those who wait for opportunities end up lying in a pile on the field while those that go for opportunities score touchdowns. If you are waiting for a new job to come, better grades, or that beautiful person to notice you, you will be a spectator for those that are going out and looking for opportunities. Could you finish your resume, contact a person for a job or talk to someone in the industry you wish to enter? Look for success opportunities today.

> "A wise man will make more opportunities than he finds"
> **- FRANCIS BACON**

> "Opportunity dances with those who are already on the dance floor."
> **- H. JACKSON BROWN**

Tip #32:
GREAT STUDENT LEADERS NEVER QUIT

"Those that give up on their dreams
disqualify themselves as leaders."

- MIKE FRITZ

I was sitting at my friend's house one day with him and his two year old son. The son was trying to climb up on the sofa and get up on its highest point (on the back of it). My buddy and I were watching this. He pulled a box over, stood on it, and climbed up on the sofa and then up to the back of the sofa and fell off. My first reaction was one of laughter ; it was hilarious. Judge me if you want but you know you might have laughed too. Following this event he was terrified of the sofa. After he settled down he walked back over to it, got back up on it, climbed up on the back of it, and put his hands in the air. Leaders never quit. It has been said that Thomas Edison tried over 10,000 times to invent the light bulb. He kept trying and trying, and then trying some more.

> "Players with fight never lose a game; they just run out of time."
> **- JOHN WOODEN**

Tip #33:
GREAT STUDENT LEADERS ACCEPT CRITICISM

I don't know about you, but accepting criticism with gratitude can be like allowing a surgeon to operate on you with no anesthesia while you just sit there and "relax." Criticism is a very hard thing to stomach, however it is crucial for a leader to handle criticism correctly. In fact, the way you handle criticism often tells people if they want to follow your leadership or not. If a teacher were to say to you, "You need to work on the way you interact in class; you are coming off very argumentative." How would you respond? If a friend said, "Man, you are so sarcastic; it gets old," how would you respond? If a coach said, "You need to change your stance," how would you respond? If a friend said, "Why do you always have to get in the last word?" what would you say? When you receive criticism like this it is an opportunity to learn and grow. Even if you don't agree with it, take any portion that may be true and seek to change.

> "Those that accept criticism are those that are truly interested in self-improvement."
>
> **- UNKNOWN**

Tip #34:

GREAT STUDENT LEADER'S AREN'T CHOSEN TO LEAD THEY CHOOSE TO LEAD.

I was never chosen to lead as a young person. In fact, I was told many times that some people have the gift of leadership and some don't ... and I was in the camp of those that don't. Because I wasn't chosen for class president, chosen to be the captain of the team or chosen for homecoming king, I assumed that I wasn't a leader. The detrimental effect of this belief is that I never tried to position myself as a leader because I "wasn't a leader." So check this out: In high school I was never chosen to lead. Look at what happened when I left school:

When I was 20 I got married
At 20 I also started my own business.

When I was 21 I built a duplex for my wife and I to live in. (We lived in half and rented out the other side. We lived for $100 a month in a brand new place.)

When I was 22 I brought on a partner because the business was growing rapidly.

At 24 I sold my company and went to college to be a pastor.

When I was 25 I took on my first church and led the student group from 5 students to 65 students in 18 months (which is unheard of growth).

When I was 26, while still in college, I received the student speaking award and spoke to our entire student body and staff (1200 people).

When I was 27 I received my bachelor's degree, finishing a 5 year program in 3 years.

When I was 27 I pastored at my second church and led for 4 years of successful ministry.

When I was 30 I received a master's degree

At 31 I started Mike Fritz Communications and became "America's Funniest Leadership Speaker".

At 32 I authored my first book.

Today I am 32 and speak nationwide.

All of this happened because I made a decision to go out and follow my dreams. Nobody chose me to accomplish any of this, I chose to accomplish it. You can do the same.

"Leaders aren't born; they are made."

- MIKE FRITZ

Tip #35:

GREAT STUDENT LEADERS CREATE A "GREENHOUSE EFFECT"

I hate yard work with a passion. The other day the leaves were on the ground (it was fall) and my wife said, "Hey you need to get those leaves up so they don't kill the grass." I thought to myself, "Yeah... kill the grass...no mowing...no bagging...no weed eating...I LOVE LEAVES."

A friend of mine owns a number of greenhouses. I was talking to him one day and he was sharing about how much work it takes to make sure the plants have the right environment in which to grow. It takes the right temperature, the right amount of sunlight, the right amount of moisture, etc. Leadership is all about creating what I call the greenhouse effect. Our job as leaders is to make it easy for followers to be personally and professionally nourished so that they have what they need to grow and change into everything thing they can be. When someone you are leading fails, you must first ask, "Did I do everything in my power to make them successful?" Then you must ask, "What can I do for him next time to help him succeed?"

> "I start with the premise that the function of leadership is to produce more leaders, not more followers."
> **- RALPH NADER**

Tip #36:

GREAT STUDENT LEADERS AREN'T DEFINED BY CIRCUMSTANCES BUT BY DECISIONS

"Responsibility comes from two words. Response and ability. When you possess responsibility you have the ability to respond any way you choose."

- STEVEN COVEY

Every day, people find themselves in circumstances that they didn't choose. Leaders see circumstances as the context for the decisions that will make them greater leaders. A few years back I received a new leadership appointment and was jacked about it. When I got there, in about 6 months I had alienated just about everybody under my leadership. I wanted to crawl in a hole and quit. I remember thinking, "I would rather just go work in a factory and not have to make any decisions that can be scrutinized." I hated every minute of it. I was watching a re-run of the Cosby show during this time and I was so emotional I began to cry. Here I am on my sofa blubbering like a baby as Cliff taught Theo how to carve a turkey. If you are laughing right now...well...you should be. It was ridiculous. My wife was next to me and tried to console me. But, seriously, I was crying over a TV show; what could she say? However, in the midst of the pain and difficulty of that leadership appointment I learned more about leadership than any other position in my life to date. It changed me as a leader and helped me lead people in a way that they bought into my leadership.

"You can't control what happens to you, the only thing you can control is how you respond."

- MIKE FRITZ

Tip #37:

GREAT STUDENT LEADERSHIP ISN'T ABOUT MOTIVATION; IT'S ABOUT ACTION

Have you ever been motivated to get a better grade in that class, get up enough nerve to ask that person out, or work hard to make the team, only to have your motivation die off before your action to achieve those things kicks in? You had so much motivation to get something done, then the next day came and your motivation was gone? Many people are motivated, but few take action. It takes motivation to take action, but many times people are motivated and then the motivation dies and they move on to something else. Leadership is about action, not some pep rally to get people cheering. What will you do the moment you put this book down today? Make a list of things you need to get done? Make a call? Make a list of goals you want to achieve in the next 5, 10, 30 or 100 days? Whatever you do, take action and do something.

"It's not enough to think positive, you need to get off your assets and take action."

- JAMES MALINCHAK

Tip #38:

GREAT STUDENT LEADERS LIVE BALANCED LIVES WITH CORRECT PRIORITIES

There is a story about a man that jumped on his horse and rode off in all directions. Have you ever felt like that? Like life is pulling you in every direction but the one you want to go? Part of leadership is the art of balancing your priorities. When you wake up tomorrow you will have homework, friends, sports, meetings, group projects, calls to make and maybe more. How do you chose what gets done and what doesn't? This is the tension of a leader. One question I ask is, "What will give me the best return on my time?" A person that makes it to the top of his business but alienates his family is not successful. A person that makes a million dollars but has no meaningful relationships has nothing.

"Allow the voices of your loved ones and your followers to be louder than any other voice in your life."

- MIKE FRITZ

Tip #39:

YOU ARE ALWAYS ONE CHOICE AWAY FROM BEING A LEADER

> "Leadership is simply a choice that places you in a position of influence."
>
> **- MIKE FRITZ**

There is no doubt people are born with different abilities. However, making decisions to place yourself in a position to influence people is not a gift, but a choice. Identifying someone who you want to influence, building a relationship so that you are in a position to influence him or her and then serving for the purpose of helping that person achieve greatness is the process of leadership. Leading is your choice.

> "Leadership is Influence"
>
> **- JOHN MAXWELL**

"Leadership isn't about position;
it's about positionING"

- MIKE FRITZ

Tip #40:

GREAT STUDENT LEADERS DO WHAT THEY TELL OTHERS TO DO

My 6 year old nephew is very observant. His parents have sought to teach him many times to resolve problems quickly. They have taught him that when someone hurts you, tell them; when you hurt others, go seek forgiveness and restore the relationship. My brother and sister-in-law (my nephew's parents) were in the middle of an argument one day and my brother-in-law walked out of the bedroom upset and went out and sat on the sofa next to my nephew. My nephew said, "Well...are you going to let this go on all night, or go in there and fix it?" Yes, a 6 year old said this. My brother-in-law smiled, got up and started walking toward the bedroom to fix the problem, and the 6 year old said, "Go get 'em, boy." After that the parents were laughing so hard they couldn't be angry at each other. There is a major hidden truth in this and it is that leaders must do what they teach others to do. As a speaker I am tested many times with the information I teach others. I teach others to serve first as leaders. So when I meet people that have the money and power to book me to speak, it is at those moments I must remember and practice what I teach, and serve others first.

> "A leader leads by example
> whether he intends to or not"
> **- UNKNOWN**

Tip #41:

GREAT STUDENT LEADERS GET BACK UP AGAIN AND AGAIN AND AGAIN

"Our greatest glory is not in never falling, but in rising every time we fall"

- CONFUCIUS

I hate getting knocked down. The summer when I was going into 4th grade was an interesting one for me. I was riding my bike around town with a friend and it just so happened to be 25-cent donut day. Donuts are delicious; I think they are proof that this truly is a good world. My friend and I came to the edge of the street and were a bit nervous because it was a busy street. So we played rock, paper, scissors to see who went first; I lost. I started across the street and rode past the first lane of traffic problem-free. But as

I entered the second lane I was hit by a pickup truck and launched into the air. After I skipped across the concrete a few times I looked down and my femur bone (thigh) was in the shape of a Z...it looked like Zorro had visited me. It took me 3 months to come back to the point that I could walk again. I was told that I would struggle running for the rest of my life. After I healed I played 4 sports in high school - football, basketball, baseball and golf. And please, no jokes about golf not being a sport. Cheerleaders and cheerleading coaches, I feel your pain. When I was told that I would struggle to run again, I could have never tried again. When we are "knocked down" by problems of life, leaders get back up, dust themselves off and keep going.

"A good man falls seven times and rises again"
- PROVERBS 24:16

Tip #42:

GREAT STUDENT LEADERS AREN'T CONSUMED BY WHAT OTHERS THINK

When I was in school I was called "spaz" more times that I can count. In the second grade I was such a lively student that my second grade teacher made a decision to put a seatbelt on my desk and strap me into it. You read that right: A SEATBELT!!!! She didn't really think that through, because as you may imagine I loved to get attention by making people laugh, so that didn't work out too well. With the new found super power of a desk strapped to my butt when I stood up, I now had the ability to do things no other student on the planet could do. One particular class period I started running with the desk strapped to me and the desk legs were banging people in the head. The teacher screamed one time, "Mike what are you doing?" to which I responded, "I am the result of your lack of thinking lady." While I loved attention, I quickly began to hate being called "spaz." It made me feel like something was wrong with me. What I didn't understand was that the energy I had would be what I one day used to entertain and motivate thousands of people throughout America. We must not let the words of people crush us and dictate our every move.

> "Don't let anybody tell you different, man: the main goal in life should always be to try to get paid to simply be yourself in your career."
> **- KEVIN SMITH**

Tip #43:

GREAT STUDENT LEADERS CREDIT OTHERS FOR THEIR OWN SUCCESS

"No man will make a great leader, who wants to do it all himself or get all the credit for it."

- ANDREW CARNEGIE

I love getting credit for things. In fact, sometimes it makes me angry when others get the credit for something that I have done. What I learned along the way in my leadership journey is that leaders do the exact opposite of that. When leading, every time we experience success we must train ourselves to ask "Who made my success possible today?" People like being made much of. When you do this it strengthens people's support of and belief in you. When people observe you recognizing others when you receive a good grade, an award, MVP on a sports team, or when you are chosen to be captain of a team, your art piece wins the contest or you win the singing competition, they gain a respect for you and see someone that doesn't see himself as self-made, but rather built and strengthened by others. People don't want to follow people who never give them recognition for a job well done.

> ### "There is no such thing as a 'self-made millionaire'"
> **- JAMES MALINCHAK**

> ### "All I am, or hope to be, I owe to my angel mother."
> **- ABRAHAM LINCOLN**

Tip #44:
GREAT LEADERS ARE FIRST GREAT FOLLOWERS

"Great leadership is earned."

- GENERAL ROBERT E. LEE

The greatest sign of leadership weakness is always having to be seen as the leader. If you are unable to be led, you can't lead. What or who are you following today in order to grow so that you can effectively lead others? The fact that you are reading this book is a good sign. Every time you seek to learn you are placing yourself in a position to be influenced by the author. Keep it up! Every chance you get, go and seek your teachers', parents', or coaches' advice and expertise so that you can become better.

"He who has not learned to obey
cannot be a good commander."

- ARISTOTLE

Tip #45:
GREAT STUDENT LEADERS ARE DECISIVE

Making decisions quickly is not the same as not thinking through issues. Decisive leadership is the art and skill of making a decision quickly, sometimes with limited information. Sometimes in leadership you make a decision based on the information that you have and then later find out you made the wrong choice. This is what leaders call normal leadership growth. Have you ever seen a speaker who is also selling a product in the back of the room? I find it so interesting to see who comes back to buy the information. You only have a few minutes to decide to buy the products and then the speaker is gone. As I have sat at my own product table the people that come back to invest in themselves have to make a quick, decisive decision to take action.

> "Leaders are decisive by nature."
> **- NAPOLEON HILL**

Tip #46:

GREAT STUDENT LEADERS ENCOURAGE THEIR FOLLOWERS REGULARLY

Nothing builds a team faster than encouragement. Think about the last time you gave a speech, sang a song, presented a piece of art work, played a good game, got a good grade, or whatever it is for you. Think about people that said, "Wow. That was a good job." Remember how you felt at that moment? The quickest way to influence someone is to encourage them. This alone won't assure people remain under your leadership for a long period of time, but it will turn the heads of those that you want to lead faster than any other method. You've got to do this one. Think about someone you can encourage right after you are done reading this book. As you are walking through the halls tomorrow, or are in your class or in your dorm, be the one that encourages people. A simple statement, "You gave a great presentation today" or "You are so gifted in _____" goes a long way. Take action right away.

"One of the indispensable principles of leadership is encouraging the hearts of your followers."

- JIM KOUZES AND HARRY POSNER

"Encouragement is the loyalty button for most people. The more you push it the more loyal they become."

- MIKE FRITZ

Tip #47:
GREAT STUDENT LEADERS TAKE RISKS

I remember sitting there signing the papers as my heart was beating rapidly. I was getting a loan to build a house that I was going to sell. If the house sold I stood to make a lot of money; if not then I was going to be stuck with a house I couldn't afford. As I walked out of the bank I hoped the loan officer didn't see the urine trail all the way to my car. I was terrified. What if it doesn't sell? What if I am stuck with a house that I can't pay for? Will I go bankrupt? These were just a few of the questions that were filling my mind. Shortly after signing the papers I started building. To make a long story short, the house sold and I made an extra $70,000 in about 6 months. Had I not taken the risk I would never have experienced the benefit. Sometimes you fail and sometimes you succeed. But the important thing is if you don't take the risk you'll never even have the chance to succeed.

"You miss 100% of the shots you don't take."

- WAYNE GRETZKY

Tip #48:
GREAT STUDENT LEADERS TAKE RESPONSIBILITY FOR FAILING

Have you ever played the blame shifting game? Isn't that a fun game? I have seen children blame the fact that they just hit someone because "they started it by hitting me first." This doesn't change when we get older. If you are driving and someone shows you their beloved tall finger, and you were to ask them, "why did you do that?" they would say something like, "Because you cut me off" or "You were driving too slow," etc. When you shift blame you are handing over your power to change; because the only person that you are able to change is yourself. You can't control what parents you are given, what teachers you have, what coaches you have, if the price of school goes up and you can't afford it. The only thing you can control is your response. When you fail a test, fail in a relationship, hurt someone, miss a shot in a game, put on an event that is a bomb, give a presentation that is terrible, don't shift blame, but own responsibility so that you can change.

> "When you shift blame, you forfeit your power to change."
>
> **- MIKE FRITZ**

Tip #49:
GREAT STUDENT LEADERS GIVE HOPE

"A leader is a dealer of hope."

- NAPOLEON BONAPARTE

Giving hope is simply helping people to see the possibilities rather than the difficulties of any given situation. I have done a lot of marriage counseling; I can tell you that most married couples are ready to go their separate ways and be done with it by the time they come to a counselor. It is my job to give them tools to change their thinking so that they can have an amazing marriage just by making some simple changes.

I've also done a lot of counseling with teens. I was sitting with a young teenager who had started cutting (a diversion strategy to free him from focusing on the problems in his life). It was amazing to see his eyes light up when I said things like, "WHEN we beat this..." and "WHEN we look back on this" and "You have to know that I have helped many people with this issue and you CAN change." To this precious young student these words were like words from heaven. Hope is essential in the leadership process. Look at the people around you who are hurting or just want to change something and seek to give them hope. Help them see the possibilities ahead of them if they take action

> "To give hope is to liberate people to see possibilities rather than obstacles."
> **- MIKE FRITZ**

Tip #50:
GREAT STUDENT LEADERS
HAVE A COACH

What do Michael Jordan, Tiger Woods, Lebron James, The San Francisco 49ers (huge fan), Justin Bieber, Donald Trump and Oprah Winfrey have in common? They all have a coach. I used to think, "What can Phil Jackson teach Michael Jordan about basketball?" or "What can Tiger Woods' caddie teach him about golf?" If you are going to lead you must have a coach. I have been speaking professionally for a long time. I still have a business coach and many other mentors. Why? It's because if I am going to be the funniest and best leadership speaker in the world I need people investing in me. My business coach is one of the best marketing and speaker coaches in the world, and even he has a coach. Which teacher, coach, parent, friend, or mentor can you enlist to be your new leadership coach? If you want to grow in the area of leadership, you can't do it on your own. I would select two people today that you will contact to ask if they will mentor and train you.

> "Leadership is not a solo flight but rather a community project."
> **- MIKE FRITZ**

Tip #51:
GREAT STUDENT LEADERS ARE TEACHABLE

Have you ever tried to teach a person who thinks that they know everything? You know: the one that says, "Oh I was just about to do that", when someone gives him an idea;" or the person that says, "I thought about that" after every suggestion that is offered to him? Isn't that annoying? Doesn't that make you want to give him a love tap on the face. I must confess that was me. I used to think that if I acted like I knew everything people would believe me and follow me. How do you respond when teachers give you suggestions on papers or projects, parents critique your ideas, or friends in your class give push back to your perspectives? How do you respond when anyone gives you a suggestion of something that you need to change?

When I was 16 years old, I was building houses with my uncle in the summers. I loved it when I learned something new and I didn't have to be taught. I began acting like I knew everything. Every time my uncle would give me guidance I would cut him off to say, "Yeah I know..." One particular time I had a project up in the rafters of the house. My uncle started to give me an idea of something that would make the project easier but I cut him off to assure him of my expertise. A few moments later I dropped a piece of wood that almost hit him, dropped and broke one of our nail guns, and was literally hanging upside down from the rafters and I could not get down. He had to come up and get me. Needless to say, I was humbled. What I found out later was that he was trying to give me help so I would understand how to walk in the rafters in a way that would keep me safe and help me avoid falling through.

Take it from me: be teachable. The guidance you might turn away in order to try to validate your own expertise might be the guidance that saves you from "hanging upside down from the rafters" of life.

> "Arrogance is one of the greatest obstacles to your leadership success."
>
> **- MIKE FRITZ**

Tip #52:

GREAT STUDENT LEADERS ARE READERS

The fact that you have read this book is a tribute to your leadership. If you are reading this, I believe you have the ability to change this world with your leadership. Never stop reading. Reading is the continual source of education that every mind can use to change the world. You are able and should be constantly working your way through a book.

Here's a 20-minute Reading Challenge: Every day when you get up, read for 10 minutes in the morning. Select something that will fuel your mind for the day. Then, right before you go to bed, again, read for 10 minutes. Once again something that will fuel your mind and your success. Don't watch a gory, killer movie right before you go to bed. When you do this

your subconscious mind chews on this all night long.
Fill your mind with world-changing information.

"You don't have to burn books
to destroy a culture. Just get
people to stop reading them."

- RAY BRADBURY

"Everything in the world exists in
order to end up as a book."

- STEPHANE MALLARME

You now have 52 tips that, one by one, you can incorporate into your life to improve as a leader. But you must act now. Don't wait until tomorrow, start today. Be inspired by reading the following thoughts from Marianne Williamson, one of the greatest leaders and achievers of our time.

OUR DEEPEST FEAR

Our deepest fear is not that we are inadequate. Our deepest fear is that we are powerful beyond measure. It is our light, not our darkness that most frightens us. We ask ourselves, Who am I to be brilliant, gorgeous, talented, fabulous? Actually, who are you not to be? You are a child of God. Your playing small does not serve the world. There is nothing enlightened about shrinking so that other people won't feel insecure around you. We are all meant to shine, as children do. We were born to make manifest the glory of God that is within us. It's not just in some of us; it's in everyone. And as we let our own light shine, we unconsciously give other people permission to do the same. As we are liberated from our own fear, our presence automatically liberates others.

- MARIANNE WILLIAMSON